The Survival G

Babies and Toddlers

By Shelley Murasko

**The guide to stress-free air travel with babies &
toddlers, including tips on in-flight entertainment,
children with special needs, and international travel**

ISBN-13:
978-1481144001

ISBN-10:
1481144006
Library of Congress Control Number: 2012907458

Library of Congress subject headings:
Family travel
Travel
Air travel
Flying with kids
Flying with toddlers
Flying with babies

Cover by Scot Ferdon
Editing by Lisa Cape Lilienthal

To my young children, Nolan & Audrey.
The aviation-enabled adventures that we have shared
have brought great joy to my life;
to my husband Mike who has given me endless
support and, most importantly, time to write,
and to my mother and father who frequently provided us
with a destination where we could land our tired wings.

Table of Contents

Introduction

Traveling with young children to visit with loved ones or to expose them to new places on this great planet is worth every bit of effort, even if that effort includes flying. With proper preparation, travel that involves flying with kids will bring joyful lifelong memories as well as many educational childhood experiences. So, congratulations for taking on the flight challenge with your young kids in tow. Let your family flight adventures begin!

In this book, you will learn everything that you need to know in order to fly stress-free with infants or toddlers. From optimizing the packing process to getting through security, from in-flight diaper changes until you step off the plane, the tips and tricks enclosed will ensure your flight success.

It's true that because of increasing security requirements and profitability challenges for airlines, flying can be one of life's most aggravating experiences. From the three mile long security lines to the three inches of in-flight legroom, the process of flying can be more than taxing for an adult flying solo. Throw young kids into the mix of flight stress and all bets are off. We're doing it, though, in big numbers. It is estimated that families traveling with small children make up 15 percent of the air travel public, leading to an estimated 64,000 parents taking flight daily around the globe with young children in tow.[9] There is no doubt that flying with children can be one of the greatest challenges you face, but only if you attempt it without knowledge and preparation. This book will give you the pointers that will ensure you not only survive but thrive while traveling with your kids.

The information shared in these pages comes from my own experiences as well as a great deal of research. I have interviewed flight attendants, airline employees, and other parents just like you and me to gather the best advice for today's families. In addition, special sections include topics like international flight pointers and flying with children who have disabilities. Lastly, I weave my personal experience throughout the book as travel has led to some of my best and worst moments as a parent. Through these stories and interviews, you will come away with the critical pointers that will lead to smooth family flight travels.

One caveat: Remember that you know your child best. While this book includes a lot of information meant to simplify the process of air travel with kids, the pointers are – in the end – simply suggestions. Never forget to trust your own judgment.

First Flight

My remedy for parenting exhaustion has always been to get help from my mom, who lives 1200 miles away. Beginning when my firstborn, Nolan, was five weeks old, we have together taken flights from San Diego to Denver to seek parental support and sanity restoration. My mom has always been a super mom. In her presence, the dishes get done, the laundry gets folded, and the children are always happy. Also, my mom and dad delight in being with their grandkids. Therefore, every trip to Grandma's is a triple win; sheer joy for the kids, for the grandparents and for me. The trick is mastering the trek and flying to Denver with what is now two very young children.

On my first trans-Rocky mountain flight, I didn't know what to expect, so to put it mildly, I overdid it. I recall over-packing my diaper bag with baby soothing tools like pacifiers, blankies, books for him, and books for me. Upon clearing security, my forehead was damp, my stomach was in knots, and I couldn't find a thing. While pacing and checking the diaper bag in the airport, I pondered what more I could buy to make the trip tolerable and sought retail therapy to soothe my anxiety. By the time we boarded and sat down, I was exhausted; and so was my son, who fell asleep for the next hour. Upon waking, he played with the tray table, safety card, plastic cup and a couple toys, and then it was time to descend. I nursed him as advised upon landing and sighed with relief as we touched ground.

As I reviewed the trip, I reflected on what caused all that undue stress. The actual flight process was significantly less severe than the one I created in my mind leading up to the trip. I noted that my anxiety was largely created by myself and my lack of knowledge of what to expect. Like so many other experiences in life, a little preparation and knowledge goes a long way to paving an easier path. So, if this is your first flight, relax. Just by reading this book, you are miles ahead of so many others.

A Travel Nightmare

On a dark chilly Christmas Eve morning, I stood at the curb of terminal 2 with my two toddlers, Nolan(2) and Audrey(1) packed in the double stroller. Anchored there by 10 pieces of luggage, I awaited the return of my husband who had gone to park the car. Airport traffic was at a standstill, and lines to our Delta flight wrapped around the ticketing counter maze, progressing at a snail's pace. As I stood there contemplating the situation, I started to panic. An inner voice percolated, warning me, "There is no way you will make your flight!" My worry kicked into overdrive, and the kids picked up on my stress and started to cry. It's amazing how observant infants are to our reactions. Panic set in and I did the only thing I could think of to do – throw money at the problem. I caught the attention of a skycap and exclaimed, "$100 to the man who can help us catch our flight." One of the skycaps must have foreseen the potential headline: "Lunatic Mom Stampedes Airport Line with Two Babies & Ton of Luggage," because a man stepped forward and said "Ma'am, calm down, I can assist. You will make your flight." To make a long story short, my husband caught up with us; and after tipping our way through the airport lines, we slid into our assigned seats without a minute to spare.

Quite often, parents will have a moment or two during family travel when their inner voice asks, "why did we think this was a good idea?" I can assure you that this is absolutely normal and will lessen as you continue to experience the joy and fun tied to your travel adventures. As a result of my mini-meltdown, I resolved to master the art of young family air travel. Not only would I study and improve the flying process, I would survive a flight alone with my toddlers and erase our travel nightmare from my memory for good. I was convinced that with the right tactics, flight with kids could be done with ease, and without necessarily emptying my wallet just to get through the airport. Let's start at the beginning: Planning your trip.

$$$ Arrive at the airport two hours in advance to avoid the temptation of costly services such as adjacent airport parking or tips for skycap heroics. $$$

Booking the Flight

At one point, while six months pregnant with baby number two and traveling with my one-year-old son cross country from Charlotte, NC, I arrived at the airport only to be told that we did not have a reservation in the system. We had awoken at 3 a.m. to drive up to Charlotte and catch a 7 a.m. flight, and during the check-in process, the agent stated, "you and your son are not among our booked passengers." I started to unravel and began to cry as the concerned agents straightened out what was an error between systems. Eventually, they found the reservation and set us up with the proper boarding pass including an infant. Fortunately, we made the flight just in time. Key learning: when flying with children, pick up the phone to book the flight accurately and completely, and follow-up with a phone call a day or two before the flight takes off.

Most airlines offer on-line booking through their websites. At all times, **I encourage you to pick up the phone to make your reservation.** It is critical to ensure that you are all booked appropriately, that seat assignments are secured, and that all of your questions are asked and answered. Spending the extra 15 minutes now will prevent major stress and save you critical minutes on flight day.

Pick up the phone while making reservations

• *Fly non-stop* whenever possible. Although multiple leg flights will often cost less, you should choose to fly non-stop in order to lessen the risk of delayed flight, to reduce your total travel time by two hours or more, and to avoid the extra hassle of deplaning and re-boarding. Airlines average 80% on-time. When they are late, they average a 50 minute delay, which means your odds of making connections on time is a gamble that can lead to being stuck overnight in an airport or strange city without luggage or baby gear.

• For short haul flights (those of three hours or less in duration) choose mid-morning flights to avoid flight delays. Morning flights average 91% on-time as opposed to 80% on-time for evening flights. In addition, children tend to be better behaved when they are less tired. It's best to aim for mid- to late- morning flights so that you arrive well-rested and have an added sense of safety that daylight brings. It is more difficult and in many cities, less safe, to be tramping around from parking lots to airport terminal in the dark with a baby. Also, by having a slightly later flight, you will be more likely to find a friend or family member who can come along to assist with the pre-flight logistics.

- For long haul flights -- flying cross-country or internationally -- it can be worth risking on-time departure to take travel in the evening when your children are more likely to sleep for the length of the flight.

- If you can, prioritize booking on airlines with the best on-time records. For on-time rates by airline in 2011 based on Bureau of Transportation and Statistics – Department of Transportation website.

As of the writing of this book, the top five airlines on-time arrival percentages were:

- Hawaiian-93%

- Alaska-89%

- Delta-89%

- Southwest-82%

- United-82%

The average arrival delay was 52 minutes.

When you call the airline and get connected to a booking agent, start the call by stating that you are booking flights for yourself and your children and specify their ages. Ask if there are any discounts or specials. "Lap children" under age two will fly free on most airlines (assuming they will sit in your lap), but you may want to consider purchasing a seat at a discount so that you can travel with a car seat. Young children tend to be safer and better behaved in the unfamiliar situation of air travel when they have the familiar environment of their own car seat.

- Ask if the airline offers any amenities for kids, such as coloring books or family movies.

- Verify what documentation you will need before boarding, including any age or identity verification for your children. For example, if you are traveling internationally and your spouse is not with you, you may need a notarized letter authorizing you to take the children outside the United States.

- Request an infant boarding pass if flying with a lap child, even if you do not pay for the child's ticket.

- Ensure seat assignments are set at time of booking and request to be seated near open seats if available. I prefer seats near the bathrooms in order to have quick access to changing tables or the "potty chair".

- Most airplanes do not have more than one extra oxygen mask per row on each side of plane. So if traveling with two adults and two lap children, make sure to book seats in pairs, so that you have one adult and one child on each side of the aisle.

- If your child is mobile, request to sit in "bulkhead" seating. Bulkhead is typically the first row of coach and allows for extra legroom and floor space where your child can move about in-flight.

  - An advantage of bulkhead is that you avoid the headache of your children wanting to kick the back of the forward seat.

  - A disadvantage of bulkhead seating is that all of your belongings – including your purse and diaper bag must be stored in the overhead compartment for takeoff and landing.

Bulkhead seating row

- Ask about baggage charges per passenger including any special deals for children (especially car seats). This might lead you to consider shipping some or all of your baggage ahead of time on USPS or UPS. At the time of this book writing, it is often cheaper to ship your luggage to your destination than pay the baggage charges.

- If your airline of choice provides the option, consider paying for "Economy Plus" when traveling with a lap child, additional $25/flight approximately. The extra 4-6 inches between seats will enable you to bend forward and utilize the tray table even with your child in your lap.

- If you are planning to take a car seat, know that the Federal Aviation Administration (FAA) requires that the car seat be placed in the window seat. Verify with the agent booking your flight so that you are assigned accordingly.

- If traveling with only a lap child (no car seat), request an aisle seat so you will have easy aisle access during flight.

- Other questions to ask:

  o   Are bassinets available on the flight? How do you reserve?

  o   Do you allow pre-boarding for families?

  o   Can we bring our stroller on board the plane?

o   Do you have diaper-changing facilities on the aircraft? (Most airplanes have one restroom with a changing table.)

o   Can an attendant warm a baby's bottle during the flight?

o   Do you offer assistance with maneuvering through the terminal when making connecting flights? How can I arrange for that?

$$$ When possible, book airline tickets with at least three weeks advance notice. Watching flight prices and signing up for price alerts on websites like Kayak.com can save you hundreds of airfare dollars. $$$

Car Seats

"Flying with a car seat is actually the only way to fly safely with a baby. Now that I've stated this, I have to qualify that commercial aviation itself is very safe and there's very little chance of anything going wrong. But if it does, your child is not protected...The FAA recently clarified its policy on car seat use. They now state that any child under the age of 18 has the right to use one... Using a car seat on board is the recommendation of the FAA, the NTSB, the AAP and other organizations including the AFA Flight Attendant union."

\- *Sharon, Flight Attendant for 13 years and mother of three http://flyingwithchildren.blogspot.com/*

Did you know that the safest place for your child on an airplane is in a government-approved child safety restraint system (CSRS) or device, not on your lap? Your arms are not capable of holding your child securely, especially during unexpected major turbulence. CSRS is defined as a hard-backed child safety seat that is approved by the government for use in both motor vehicles and aircraft. FAA controls the approval of some but not all CSRS, and not all car seats are approved for use in airplanes. Make sure your CSRS is government approved and has "This restraint is certified for use in motor vehicles and aircraft" printed on it. Otherwise, you may be asked to check the CSRS as baggage.

Small children tend to fly better in car seats where they know they must stay seated. If you have purchased an extra seat or the airline implies extra seats, take the car seat with you to the gate. Most airlines will attempt to accommodate you with an empty seat in which case, the car seat will enable the likelihood of infant sleep and contentment.

A few pointers on car seats:

• They must be FAA approved – check underside of seat and note that the flight attendants are supposed to check for the FAA approval as well.

FAA Approval label required on car seats

• The FAA has banned use of supplemental lap restraints,

or "belly belts", in airplanes. Booster seats and harness vests may be used during flight, but not during taxi, takeoff, or landing. Your airline may or may not enforce these rules.

• You must have an additional seat on the plane in which to place your car seat – if an extra seat is not available (and you have not paid for a seat for your child), the airline will "gate check" your car seat at the departure gate, which means it will be tagged and sent to the belly of the plane with the rest of the luggage. If that's the case, you will need to pick it up when you deplane as you exit the aircraft.

• If you are traveling alone, make sure to ask the flight attendant for help as you step into the plane. Car seats along with diaper bag and baby are difficult to carry up the narrow airplane aisle, and most flight attendants are happy to help because it will speed the boarding process along.

• One final recommendation on car seats comes from my good friend, Emily Nelson, who just completed six hours of flying alone with her two toddlers: "If you have two or more kids, it's worth taking a car seat on board. You'll end up putting the "lap child" – the smaller, wiggly child -- in the car seat and putting your older child on your lap!"

> $$$ Car seats can be checked for free; so as long as you have a way to transport one into the airport, bring your own versus paying to rent one at your

destination. $$$

Gate Passes

After my first flight alone with my children, we safely landed in Denver and came off of the airplane only to be pleasantly surprised to see Grandma and Grandpa waiting patiently for us with big smiles right there at the gate. What a relief, help was there; and we were in good hands. This is when my parents shared with me how easy it was to ask for a gate pass from the airline with very few questions asked.

One secret of many airports is that they will allow airlines to issue family gate passes to adults assisting minors to or from the gates. ***Most airlines are pretty flexible about issuing gate passes when children are involved.*** I would not count on a spouse or friend securing a gate pass to assist you through security, but as long as the airport is not too crowded, the gate passes are often granted.

Thus, it is worth trying; and from conversations with Southwest and American Airlines public relations teams, I learned that they are commonly issued upon request as long as the airport is not overwhelmed with travelers. It is not always a guarantee, however, as I learned recently when my parents were denied a pass on a busy Monday morning at Denver airport. I suspect that if they would have approached the counter apart from me and the kids and stated that they needed passes to help with minors, they would have received the passes. When traveling alone with two kids, it is worth the request to seek a gate pass for a family member to assist you. If your family member or friend does request a gate pass, they will need to show an I.D. and pass through security, just as though they are traveling.

$$$ If unable to travel with assistance within the airport, simply ensure you have as many hands-free travel items as possible such as a Baby Bjorn, large backpack, and/or stroller with storage space. Most items can be purchased for half the price on Craigslist or Ebay. $$$

Getting to the Airport

Running late to the airport, I quickly parked the car in the long term parking lot. After pulling into the parking spot, I got out of the car and unloaded my suitcase, carry-on, car seat, stroller, and laptop bag. Then, I had the realization, "how am I going to get all of this gear from my car into the airport with only one hour to go before flight?" Luckily, at that moment, my guardian airport transport bus magically appeared with a very helpful driver and no other passengers on board.

The most difficult step in traveling alone with a baby can be the travel to and from the terminal and airport parking. Every airport is different, but in many cases there is a fair distance between short or long term parking and the terminal. You should strategize in advance how you will get you, your baby, your luggage, stroller and car seat back and forth if you are traveling alone. Some options to consider:

• Arranging for a reliable friend or family member to take you to and from the airport and bypass the extra hassle altogether. Your driver should be able to drop you off at curbside check-in, or near the ticketing counter at the airport, minimizing the distance you'll travel with baby and gear in tow.

- Pay a higher parking rate and park in daily or short term parking, so that you will be able to walk with your stroller and roller bag from your car into the airport terminal without having to take a bus.

- If the airport has a shuttle system, it is worthwhile to call ahead of time and find out their policies for helping parents who are flying alone with small children. Some services may be very helpful and pick you up right by your car; whereas, others might require you to walk a ways to get to their bus stop. Also, find out how often their shuttles circulate the airport.

- At larger metropolitan airports, consider the off-site park and ride lots such as Wally Park or The Parking Spot. While these services charge a premium, the benefits include a shuttle bus and driver who will help you load and unload, door to door. If you choose to use a park and ride, look for discounts online ahead of time.

    For times when you are traveling alone with your child, the following tips apply:

- Ensure you have allowed extra time to transport from parking to the terminal, depending on the airport this might mean building in 30 minutes or more.

- Allow shuttle drivers to do all the heavy lifting – focus completely on handling your children.

- Hand over your stroller to the shuttle driver last if your children are sitting in it.

- Make note of your parking spot and store the note in your wallet or your smart phone.

- Tell the shuttle driver which airline you are using.

- Have your hands free and be prepared to hold children securely on the shuttle rides as most shuttles will not have seatbelts.

  - $$$ Search airport parking options on-line ahead of time to ensure lowest cost option. Parking at the adjacent short term parking for large airports can cost one upwards of $20/ day. $$$

Lighten Your Baggage

"Simplicity is making the journey of this life with just baggage enough."

- *Charles Dudley Warner*

Ideally, you fly with nothing other than your child, your carry-on/diaper bag, and an umbrella stroller or carrying device (like Baby Bjorn). This takes some planning (and pruning) but will be well worth the hassle as you maneuver from the parking lot, through the terminal, through security lines, to the gate, onto the airplane, and every step in reverse upon arrival. When I spoke with Trish MacDonald of American Airlines and asked for her one and only best tip for parents it was simply, "Don't over pack". How might you be a traveling minimalist with kids in tow? Here are some suggestions:

- Pack Less! This is not the time to decide you need a different pair of shoes for every outfit that you wear on your trip, so pack light. Be ruthless -- after packing what you think you will need for the trip, go back and force yourself to unpack five or more of those items. You may even decide early on that you are going to do laundry during your travel and cut your clothing needs in half.

23

- ***Lighten your load by shipping luggage ahead of time.*** Pack a box of items needed at your destination and ship it ahead of time. Most hotels & destination points will receive and store your luggage upon your request. Larger boxes that weigh 20 pounds or more will often be least expensive flown via USPS Parcel Post, but you will need to allow at least seven business days for delivery. FedEx Ground is also quite competitive for large box shipments. It would be worth checking the websites for USPS, FedEx Ground, and UPS rates to get the cheapest shipping option. Do not forget to add insurance; it will cost you a little extra but is worth it in case a package gets lost.

  o   If money is no object, consider going with a service by a company that specializes in shipping luggage such as Luggage Free or Luggage Concierge. It will cost more, but there will be advantages such as: more personal attention, better handling in the case of major flight delays, and overall door to door service.

  o   A second advantage of shipping luggage ahead is that it will allow you to choose 'baggage free' check-in lines at the airport that are often shorter. This applies only if you are not traveling with a lap child. With a lap child, you will need to check in at the ticket counter with an agent.

  o   Lastly, a final advantage of this approach is that

it will force you to plan ahead and relieve yourself of having to worry about packing the week of departure. It is amazing how much less stress is involved in travel when your packing and luggage handling are done ahead of time, thus the day before flight your main concerns are the carry-on bag and a good night's sleep.

• If you must check baggage at the airport, make sure you pack suitcases that require only one hand to easily maneuver. Rolling duffels are ideal for hooking car seats to the handle. If you are traveling with additional items such as a bike or skis, consider shipping ahead of time via UPS.

Go-Go Babyz Car Seat Luggage

• Beg, Borrow, and Rent at Your Destination. You should plan ahead to borrow or rent items at your destination to prevent having to pack them. Most hotels will equip rooms with baby cribs or pack-n-plays. Car rental agencies will rent

25

car seats for $5-10 per day, and this fee can be negotiated. Family members may be willing to borrow cribs or car seats from neighbors. Businesses now exist that will provide baby's needed items at destination such as pack-n-plays, strollers, car seats, etc. Use Google to search for baby gear rentals in your destination city. Two popular options are: Baby's Away and Baby-Equipment-Rental.com. Often times, they will even deliver needed items to local hotels.

- Practice being a human cargo rack before the day of flight. Yes, I mean, literally. Practice walking from your house to the end of driveway with all expected travel items such as the rolling suitcase, stroller, carry-on backpack, and, oh yes, your child.

$$$ Ensure your bag weighs no more than 50 lbs or you will pay for the excess weight. $$$

Three Days Prior to Takeoff

Calling all procrastinators! This chapter is included to encourage you to complete all needed actions to prep for your flight well before takeoff. It is too easy to procrastinate and end up running around finalizing all details the day before flight, which will only lead you to be exhausted on the Big Day. I want you to feel rested, relaxed and prepared before flight. Hence, the mandatory Three Days Prior Prepared Parent Checklist:

☑ Complete all laundry that will be needed for your trip.

☑ Complete all errands for items needed for the trip.

☑ Prepare all luggage that will be needed ahead of time.

☑ Create a packing checklist.

☑ Pack all items that are not needed in the coming days.

☑ Transfer strollers and carriers to the car.

☑ Fill up car with gas.

☑ Print off all directions needed for navigation.

☑ Practice maneuvering all luggage and bags to ensure transportability.

Carry-on Packing List

A carry-on bag should have plenty of room for all necessary in-flight items. My recommendation is a comfortable backpack larger than a typical diaper bag. Pockets are helpful, too, in keeping items organized, as long as you can remember which pockets hold key items. Remember, you must be able to fit the carry-on under an airplane seat and thus know that the 22" long x 14" wide x 9" tall are the maximum dimensions allowed.

☑ *If you are worried about ear pressure there are great ear plugs called Kids Earplane Ear Plugs* – according to one parent: "they make them for children and adults. They work, and they are awesome!"

☑ Food snacks. Think fun, yummy, different, and time-consuming, with some consideration to sugar content. Examples: cookies, large suckers, bottled water in fancy squirt bottle, Cheetos, teething biscuits, bubble gum, fruit wraps, beef jerky (just kidding, but I'm sure you get my point). Make sure to include at least one 'favorite' per child for every 30 minutes of flight and plan to pace the distribution of treats.

☑ Documents

    o   International – Passport for all passengers

- Domestic – Bring birth certificates for age verification

☑ Wallet, ID, itinerary, boarding passes (after checking in on-line the day before)

☑ Lots of Diapers (I mean **lots!**), wipes, a change of clothes

☑ In case of vomit or blow-outs, extra shirt for mom & dad

☑ Pacifier, bottles, sippy cups, curly straws – items that will foster sucking upon takeoff and landing

- Please note – you may not take containers through security with more than 3.4 ounces (100 mL) of liquid. It is best to travel with cups and bottles empty, and then fill them after passing through security.

☑ Entertainment for the plane –see next section – at least one fun item per child for every 15 minutes preferably wrapped with paper.

☑ Baby Benadryl for allergies, Baby Motrin for teething pain. Consult with your doctor for other suggestions.

☑ Token of appreciation for lucky passengers who get to sit next to you during flight such as earplugs or wrapped candy.

$$$ Ensure all carry-on bags are under 22" long x 14" wide x 9" tall to avoid having to check additional items and incur additional baggage fees. $$$

In-Flight Child Entertainment

When my son was 18 months old, we took flight with a diaper bag carefully packed with interesting objects and favorite toys. Much to my surprise he was most entertained by the tray table that folds into the arm of the airplane chair when you sit in the bulkhead row. For at least a half hour, he simply wanted to see me fold the tray table in and out of the armrest over and over about 50 times. Who knew a tray table could be quite so mesmerizing?

Only you know what items will entertain your child the most; and often times, toy 'interests' are unique to each child. Observe toys that capture attention for five minutes or more, and include those items or add new versions of those toys. With that said, there are some recommended items below that seem to consistently entertain. **You are encouraged to include at least one play item for every 15 minutes in flight and plan on rotating and pacing your child with the items.** Since your child will be in constant supervision, you can often times find household items that they will find interesting that wouldn't normally qualify as 'safe' toys such as a roll of tape or teaspoons. **You can make this even more interesting and time consuming for the child by wrapping the** *items in paper (now they have something to draw on, too); and make sure to mix in a few 'new' things.*

Once your child is age two or older, they may find iPhone or iPad apps or movies entertaining. Just make sure to provide really good headphones so as not to upset the passengers around you. One you may want to consider: **Kidz Gear Wired Headphones For Kids by Kidz Gear available on Amazon.**

If you don't have time to pull together toys and have them wrapped, go to eBay and order a kid's "Jetpack" from Mama_On_The_Go, a small age-appropriate goodie bag for family travel.

Fisher Price Doodle Pro OR Ebay Jetpack by Mama_On_The _Go

Babies

- Favorite rattle

- Small toy with music/lights

- Infantino animals (crinkle paper, mirrors, sounds)

- Crinkle paper toys or books available on Amazon

- Keys

- Teaspoons

- Blue painter's tape to stick to tray table and unstick

- Touch and feel books

- Your rested singing voice and in-seat dance moves

- New baby toys like a baby cell phone

Kids 1-2

- Wax sticks (Bendaroos or WikiStix). They stick to the tray table and are fun.[4]

- Ribbons made of different fabrics

- Slinky

- Cars and tractors

- Michaels craft store goodies

- Inexpensive toys from Target's or Walmart's dollar section

- Colored paper clips connected together

- Tiny flashlight

- Wind-up toys that make mild noises

- Lock & key

- Lap games: patty cake, row/row/row your boat

- Hold them so they can see other passengers

- Walk to back of plane for change of environment

- Airplane items: plastic cup, window shade, food tray, safety card

- Finger puppets (including hand drawn faces on your fingers)

- iPad with videos, music and photos of your family and child

- Stickers and/or sticker book

- Prior to flight allow the 'active' child to have plenty of play time in the terminal – many airports now have indoor kids play areas

Kids 2 years and above:

- Small DVD player or iPad to show one or two favorite

movies. Note that movies will need to be downloaded well in advance of travel, as the onboard wi-fi (for which you will pay between $5-15 if available) will not be high speed enough to accommodate downloads in-flight.

- Age appropriate iPhone apps such as Bubble Pop, Wheels on the Bus, and Thomas the Train

- There's an app for just about everything, so think about your child's special interests and download ahead of time.

- Bob the Builder Imaginetics magnet set

- Crayola wonder markers – they color only on special paper that is provided, thus less worry about clean-up

- Magnadoodle- mini or large by "Parents" brand

- Little cars/tractors/ buses

- Little dolls

- "Create A Scene" magnetic playset like the construction site

- Special books – pop ups, magnetic fish, stickers

- Puzzles

- Carry-on backpack with zippers or pockets

- Favorite travel buddy like stuffed teddy bear or doll

- For little girls, lip gloss or powder from mom's purse can become a makeshift princess game

$$$ Make travel purchases ahead of time, including a few soothing devices for mom or dad such as a magazine, favorite snack, or portable music. Purchasing anything in the gift stores at the airport will cost you. $$$

Day Before

"When preparing to travel, lay out all your clothes and all your money. Then take half the clothes and twice the money." -- Susan Heller

The most important item to take with you on your flight is your own rested, healthy, satisfied, calm self. There is no room for bad moods when flying with small children. So, do everything that you can to get a full night of sleep before takeoff.

Before you nod off to sleep, there are a few helpful steps to take to set your mind at ease:

• Check for flight delays by calling the airline or entering your flight number on their website.

• ***Check in ahead of time on the airline's website*** (doesn't apply when traveling with a lap child).

• Double-check that you have all essentials in the diaper bag: diapers, wipes, spare clothes, entertainment items fully charged, toys, books, snacks, formula, pacifier, cups.

• Set out all luggage and carry-ons in one location, and pre-load the stroller and extra car seats into the car.

• Contact whoever is picking you up at your destination to

double check that they have the correct flight arrival time and coordinate a meeting point.

- Create a short list of items to pack on flight day that you need to use over the night such as:

  o Blankets

  o Pacifiers

  o Toiletries

  o Medications

  o Sound machine (if child is used to sleeping with sound device it might be worth packing if it will fit)

- Set out clothes for the kids and yourself.

  o Consider dressing the kids in dressier clothes than normal to make a good impression. Also, ensure they will be comfortable and warm. For early morning or evening flights, pajamas might be appropriate and may also lead to a good nap on the plane.

  o *Also, ensure plenty of layers to enable warmth or cooling upon a moment's notice. Airplanes and airports can fluctuate in temperature.*

The key message here as my mother always told me, "Do not put off for tomorrow, that which can get done today."

Morning of Takeoff

"Keep Calm and Carry On."

-poster produced by United Kingdom

Government prior to World War II

Ah, you awake feeling energized and rested. You can take on just about anything the day brings. Here are some final things to consider:

✓ Allow children to sleep in as much as possible.

✓ All travelers should eat a healthy meal before flying.

✓ Complete all final packing on your "same day packing list".

✓ Check flight departure time on-line or by calling the airport.

✓ Ensure all luggage, strollers, car seats are in the car; and do one final driver's license/credit card/flight information check before hitting the road.

Check-In

"What a nightmare! In the process of flying my infant and toddler from Boise through Denver to Dallas, I realized at security that my boarding pass was missing "INF," the code that indicates you are traveling with a lap child who does not have their own pass. Immediately, I returned to the check-in counter to have this corrected. Bear in mind, I am traveling alone with a double stroller, a car seat, a large carry-on, and two young children. The ticketing agent could not figure out how to re-print the boarding pass with INF, so she decided to delete the reservation and re-book. As a result, she wasn't able to re-book the Denver leg of the flight; and we were told we had five minutes to immediately board the plane to Denver or we would miss the flight. I quickly reviewed my options: stay back in Boise where at least I would be stuck with my parents who had driven us three hours to the airport, or take the leap of faith that things would work out. Panicked, I decided to go for it; and we ran to the gate. Luckily, before takeoff, I texted my husband, reached him, and asked him to sort things out while we were in the air. Upon landing, I learned he had been successful; and we were all set with the Dallas flight. What a relief!"

-Emily Nelson, mother of 2 toddlers & experienced flight passenger

Once you arrive within the terminal, expect to see lines. Usually, there are flight attendants guiding people, so communicate with them and ensure you are in the right line. Mention to them that you will need an infant's boarding pass, if that is the case; and ask if there is a family line for check-in. By communicating and ensuring that they see you alone with children (I know...how can they not?), they will be more likely to share a shortcut, maybe even walk you to the front of the line. While you are snaking your way through the line, ensure all documents are within reach for check-in. Usually, at this point, the kids are pretty content to observe all the people, luggage, and activity.

Once you reach the counter, you will follow all standard check-in procedures. Slide credit card or enter confirmation number into the kiosk, and proceed through questions as you are prompted. *Talk with the counter agent to ensure you have the correct boarding documents, including an infant boarding pass, a pass with the letters INF, if appropriate.*

Communicate clearly the items which will need to be checked, and watch with glee as they get loaded off your shoulders and onto the conveyor belt. Be very conscious of where you put your tickets, driver's license, and baggage claim receipts. Keep them handy and together in a secure place. You will need identification and boarding passes as you go through security. Now, proceed to security.

$$$ Watch how baggage fees are assessed during check-in. It might be less costly to select one bag per ticketed passenger than to add three bags to your ticket alone. $$$

AAAaargh, TSA! Getting Through Security

"Lady with the baby! Lady with the baby!"
announced the TSA agent as I was standing in a
long line with my newborn. Once the agent finally
broke through my nervous gaze, I grinned with
relief as he motioned for me to move to the front of
the long line. —

Robyn Mott, Mother of two and experienced traveler

TSA stands for Transportation Security Administration. Though some people find security to be the most difficult part of airport logistics, the agents can be helpful if you give them a chance. Once you arrive at the security line, make sure to make eye contact and smile at the agents. If they still seem to ignore the fact that you are traveling with young children; then when you get within earshot, ask kindly if they have a family friendly line. Even if this line appears slightly longer, your baby or toddler will appreciate having other kids to watch while waiting in line.

If you do remain in a long line for whatever reason, simply remain cheerful and calm. Recite to yourself, "You will not miss your flight." As you wait in line, think through all the steps you will take once you get to the scanner and what you will do. Your focus should be on keeping your kids content and placing all items on the TSA security belt appropriately.   Remember that you will not be required to separate from your children, though the agents might instruct you to carry the kids rather than use a baby carrier. Here are some pointers to help you avoid any extra screening hassle:

- Your shoes must be removed, but children's can stay on.

- Laptops and tablets need to be taken out of carry-on bags and placed separately through the scanners.

- The item that you are using to carry your child should be the last thing you remove to add to the conveyor, but the first thing you put through the scanner so you will have it first on the other side. Strollers can be a tight fit through the conveyor belt; but if folded up properly, they are usually able to get through with a little push. After removing all items from stroller pockets, make sure the stroller is completely collapsed.

- Liquids – you are allowed one small quart size bag for your personal items; but if carrying a child you are allowed an extra gallon sized bag for sippy cups, formula, diaper cream, and wipes. To prevent delay, you should leave cups or bottles free of liquid until passing through security. If carrying liquid in the bottles and cups, the agents will likely want to test them. This is time-consuming and a little complicated, so avoid it if you can.

- Jackets and sweaters need to be removed from all parties.

- Human X-ray scan

    o   You will be allowed to carry your child through the x-ray and to keep your infant in a carrier.

    o   Another option, if conducive to the child, is to have them walk through the x-ray scan on their own. Before age three, I was unable to get my son to do such a thing, so my approach was to carry both children at the same time.

- *If you feel like you cannot reasonably carry your kids through the x-ray scan or have them pass through on their own, then indicate to TSA that you want a private screening.*

And, once you are through, congratulations! Managing the TSA process can be taxing to say the least. I normally do a quick happy dance after passing through, which serves the kids well, too!

$$$ Ensure that you do not take any items through security that will get confiscated such as large bottles of hairspray, a bottle of balsamic vinegar, small scissors, or mace. These are all items that I have mistakenly carried with me during past travels that resulted in some financial loss when security took them away. $$$

In the Airport prior to Takeoff

Each child has their unique interests and talents. My son has always been interested in machines. Thus, it worked quite well to find a glass elevator at the Salt Lake City Airport that he enjoyed watching for about an hour. Up and down, up and down, Up and down....

Make the most of any remaining time that you have left before takeoff. If you have a family member assisting you through the airport with use of a gate pass, let them handle the bulk of the in airport responsibility while you take time to use the restroom, pass by the gift store for final self-medication, and take some deep breaths. When there is limited time to spare, follow these steps:

Priority 1: **The gate.** Find your gate.

Priority 2: **Boarding time.** Confirm what time the attendant expects to board you. If you are with two children or several overhead bags, you will want to take advantage of the family first pre-boarding, so ask when that will occur. If checked all luggage, and it is only you, your child, and one carry-on, I suggest being one of the last ones to board. It is much easier to keep a child content and entertained in the airport than on the airplane for an extra 20 minutes.

Priority 3: **Stroller tag.** If taking a stroller on the plane, you should request a stroller tag from a gate agent. You will not be allowed to take the stroller onto the plane in most cases, but you can take it all the way through the boarding process up until you step onto the plane. From there, your stroller will be taken down to the belly of the plane, and you will be given a claim slip. Note whether it is a "gate claim" or a "baggage claim" – if it is a gate claim, it will be waiting at the boarding door when you disembark. If it is a baggage claim, you won't be able to retrieve it until you get to the baggage area. The preference is a gate claim.

Priority 4: **Bathroom & water.** Hit the restrooms for final diaper checks/changing and chance for you to release your bladder. Refill sippy cups with water or favorite beverage.

If you are a mom traveling with your husband, make sure to give him ample time to carry the baby. When moms carry babies around airports (or airplanes for that matter), they are often stared upon like three-headed monsters. When dad carries a baby in a Bjorn or walks hand in hand with a toddler, they are regarded like heroes of the highest order. You don't want your husband to miss out on that glory, do you?

$$$ Avoid full service restaurants as it will be useful to allow your toddler time to walk or crawl around while they can, and it will save you a few bucks as well. $$$

The Flight

"My son, Pax, rests. For about a minute.
Then....BWAAAAP. 'Whoa,' I think. 'It sounds like Pax just
threw up? But no. That can't be'. Then I feel it: Great,
big, warm chunks of vomit....soaking my back. Shocked, I
pull Pax away and look at him, 'Buddy! Are you OK?' Pax
answers by throwing up in my lap... But, Pax wasn't
finished. In desperation, I hold up my one free hand, which
he promptly fills with more puke. Now God knows I've been
puked on before. A bunch. But never have I been So.
Totally. Soaked. with puke. Down my back. Down my
front. Pooling in my lap. And filling my hand... 'PRESS
THE CALL BUTTON!!!' I yell at the guy sitting next to me,
who has jumped up in shock. Instead, he runs down the
aisle and returns with....ready for this one? TWO
KLEENEX. Not two boxes, but two tiiiny, thin pieces of
Kleenex."

-Shana Draugelis, the Draugelis Blog, The One Where
Get A Smack Down in the Air, May 201

Upon boarding, you will greet your flight attendants wit
a relaxed and confident smile. Flight attendants receive ver
little training on supporting parents with kids; but in

general, they are there to help and most will attempt to assist you with your requests. One flight attendant I interviewed, Trish McCarthy, mentioned "although we are discouraged in training from carrying passenger items such as bags or car seats, if you need help and ask, we will help." *If you are traveling alone with two children, you will likely need a little assistance carrying a car seat, so don't hesitate to ask.*

As the plane is boarding, talk with an available attendant about your child's safety. They can offer you input on how to handle emergencies. Introduce yourself to fellow passengers, especially in your aisle. You might consider buying them a beverage or passing around some candy if it helps garner their support for whatever the flight might entail.

In the final moments before takeoff, the flight attendants will request that all electronics are turned off. This is a good time to get out the first snack, or to start nursing/bottle-feeding your child. *It is critical that your child chews or sucks during takeoff or landing; and this will also provide them with something to do while electronics must remain powered off.* So, make sure you present several options to get them chewing: sucker, gummy teddy bears, fruit snacks, nuts, favorite bars.

For mothers that are nursing, nurse your baby during takeoff and landing. If you are on a short flight, then use a pacifier for takeoff and nurse upon landing. Obviously, you want to ensure that you have a nursing cover with good coverage, and burp cloth. Formula may be another option, so be prepared with bottles and formula powder; flight attendants can sometimes bring lukewarm water upon request. If you explain the purpose of the water, many attendants will know how to provide water at a satisfactory temperature for your baby. As always, test the water temp yourself to ensure it is adequate.

As the attendants do final pre-flight checks, talk to your toddler about the airplane takeoff and what to expect. You may describe that the pilot will drive the plane around for a while on the runway. Then, the plane will start to go fast and get very loud. Also, mention that they may feel a tickle or itch in their ear that will soon go away. The more you can show your child that things are going as expected, the more likely they will be to remain calm and relaxed.

There are going to be times during flight when the child must remain in their seat, and the seatbelt sign will be displayed. So, you may want to give your child extra time to crawl around before takeoff. Also, be prepared to turn-off electronics upon take off, including laptops, tablets, and cell phones. This will be a good time to start offering the first special treat or snack.

If your toddler is in their car seat (which is strongly encouraged as it is a place they are accustomed to sitting), **use an airplane blanket as a sling or safety net to catch toys or pacifiers that drop or get thrown during flight.** Place one end of the blanket under the car seat and the other end tucked into the seat pocket in front of them. When a toy gets thrown or a crayon gets dropped, the blanket will catch all items and make your life a lot easier. It can be difficult to pick items up from the airplane floor, and clean up after a long flight can be a disaster. But, with this handy airplane blanket technique, you will save yourself effort and impress fellow passengers.

Once in flight, pass out your wrapped toys and treats at a pace of one per fifteen minutes. *Inevitably, you will encounter a minor meltdown or a moment where your toddler might say, "Mommy, I am done with the airplane." When this occurs, the very best step is to take a walk and change up the scenery a bit. The back galley of the plane can provide a nice break from the limited space in rows.* Another option is giving your child the chance to look around and wave at others. Who knows, maybe there will be a grandma two rows back waving and making funny faces. Also, you can talk with a flight attendant for a suggestion. Some of the more seasoned flight attendants may offer assistance if requested such as giving special airline 'wings,' tablets & pens, or a special snack. It never hurts to ask. As a parent, you might think of something creative on the fly such as a new little song while lap-bouncing or a pretend 'princess' game including use of your sacred purse items like face powder or lip gloss. Most importantly, stay calm and try a new idea.

Although it is challenging to fly with little ones, do not allow this fact to become an excuse for letting your child disrupt other passengers' trips. One very common behavioral challenge might be your toddler kicking the back of the chair of the person in front of them. Though it may be difficult, you should try to distract your child from doing this. Communication with the other passenger might also be helpful. Simply let them know that you are sorry and that you are trying to get your child to stop. And, then take appropriate steps to deter the action. Distraction can be effective such as a quick walk around the airplane.

$$$ Take advantage of every free item offered during flight as you never know what might serve to entertain, but avoid purchasing in-flight services sold at a premium. $$$

Restroom / Diaper Changes

Upon take off to Florida, our 8-month-old son had a blowout diaper. We remained seated until the "Seatbelts Required" sign turned off and then quickly walked up to the restroom for a change. Fortunately, we had carried extra diapers and clothes, for my son was covered in poop from the waist down. Also, it was all over my sleeve, and smelled sooooooooo lovely. After 10 stinky minutes in the restroom cleaning him up and rinsing my sleeve in the sink, followed by 15 minutes laughing at ourselves, we relaxed in our seats feeling almost normal.

Overall, airport changing facilities have come a long way and should meet most of your diaper changing needs. Most airport restrooms will offer changing tables; and in addition, family restrooms may be available in family friendly airports. Handicapped restroom stalls are a good option in the case that you need to use the bathroom while keeping your child with you for they will accommodate a stroller up to the size of most double strollers. Remember, that while you are using the stall, there may be someone waiting who has no other option than to use that stall. Keep your visit quick!

Unlike diaper changing in the airports, changing a child's diaper in the airplane restroom is like changing a diaper inside a refrigerator box. Most airplanes will have a small changing table in the cramped restroom near the front of the plane. Upon boarding, check with the flight attendant to confirm which restroom has the changing table. If the airplane does not have a changing table, your diaper change options are limited to using the closed toilet seat in the cramped bathroom. *In the event that you have two children or more traveling with you and a diaper change is warranted, a flight attendant will assist you with staying with your other children or standing with a child while you use the restroom[2].*

Airplane restroom – changing table opens above toilet

Eventually, you will face a blowout diaper during a takeoff or landing when you can't get out of your seat. It is important that safety take priority and that you remain in your seat. Attempting to change a diaper in your lap or adjacent airplane seat is discouraged. You never know how severe the diaper will be; and fellow passengers will deal better with a little stink than a full-blown view of a diaper change. I have been tempted to change the child in my lap; but after speaking with several fellow passengers and flight attendants, the minor stink is preferable for 15-30 minutes is preferable.

Upon Arrival

My sister Robyn exposed me to the stress of young family travel before I had children of my own. We stood at the baggage claim in Des Moines airport with her two sons, watching the same suitcases circling around like a broken record. Clearly, their bags had gone missing, and my sister's stress barometer slowly shot up to maximum. Smoke steamed from her ears as we rolled the stroller over to the baggage attendant's counter. She leaned in towards the attendant and demanded, "Where is my luggage?" The attendant was unprepared for my sister's demeanor and rattled off their standard phrases..."they will be delivered as soon as they are located" "we apologize for the inconvenience." My sister became madder and meaner, and her response that day may have led the agent to reconsider her career choice.

After your first flight with children, it will feel like a relief to land and get off the plane. ***If you are traveling with more than one child, it may be easier to be the last one off of the plane.*** Most likely, you will have to wait for your checked luggage anyway, so taking your time getting of the plane can prove helpful.

Another advantage of being last off the plane is that you will have plenty of time to ensure that you have retrieved all your belongings.

Right before you exit the airplane, take a moment to thank the flight crew for the safe flight and extra assistance that they offered. Not only will this be good karma for you, but it might lead to improved handling and support of other families who will board.

Lastly, do not forget to retrieve your stroller as you deplane. As you load your child and bag into the stroller, take a moment to sigh with relief, the hard part is over. Then, find the nearest restroom and proceed to baggage claim. If for some reason, your luggage is lost, see the agent near the baggage area. They will ask to see your luggage tags and will work on tracking down your bags. Most likely, if they are missing or in another city, the airport will have them delivered within 24 hours. So, though it is annoying not to have your bags when you leave, look on the bright side, it is one less thing to have to carry and load. If you are missing your car seat and need to leave the airport, proceed to a Hertz or Avis rental car counter. *They will occasionally rent car seats even if you are not renting a car.*

$$$ Before exiting the plane, do a double check for items such as cell phone, wallet, luggage tags, keys, pacifier, special

blankie, and anything else that is of particular value to you.

$$$

International Flight

"Twenty years from now you will be more disappointed by the things you didn't do than by the ones you did do. So throw off the bowlines, sail away from the safe harbor. Catch the trade winds in your sails. Explore. Dream. Discover."

– Mark Twain

Flying internationally with young children offers some additional considerations. Listed below are some of the unique aspects of international travel that are essential to know:

Special documentation is needed:

- Passport for every child.

All children are required to have a ticket for international flights, though most infant tickets are discounted.

According to a fellow parent, Emily Nelson:

"Depending on where you are going you may need to have your child vaccinated. Don't forget their vaccine card."

Most all airlines offer special seating for families:

Reserve flights early and request bulkhead seating with bassinet, ideally in the center of the plane or in a window seat.

- If "bulkhead" is not assigned upon booking the flight, then take steps to secure it at the airport. Arrive at the airport more than two hours early, and ask the ticketing agent.

- ***If still not assured of the "bulkhead" row, then proceed to your gate at least one hour before the flight takes off and ask the gate agent.***

- If flying with an infant, make sure to ask for a bassinet.

Bassinets in the bulkhead row

Questions to remember at time of booking ticket include:

- What do they charge for lap babies under 2?
- Are there seat discounts for children under 2?
- Can my child sit in his own car seat?
- What documentation is required?
- Do all rows have extra oxygen masks?
- Do lap babies have a baggage allowance?
- Can they have a carry-on?
- Are children's meals included? Are any snacks offered?
- Are there changing tables on the airplane?
- Can my spouse or loved one get security clearance to accompany me to the departure gate if I need assistance?

For international flights, many of the previous domestic ips apply. Some additional tips include:

- Fly during the night whenever possible.
- Consult with a doctor for options to facilitate sleep or ase ear pain during takeoff.

Securing a passport can prove problematic if not handled at least three months prior to travel. And, remember, all children are required to have a passport o fly internationally. The easiest way to secure a passport is o call your post office and set up an appointment. Both parents are required to be present when a child's passport is issued. Kids' passports are valid for five years.

Family-Friendly Airlines

Who is the ultimate family-friendly airline? Great question. I wish I had a great answer. I personally do not see any airline attempting to target the family market, especially within the United States. It is likely a business decision; rather than an indication of their interest in supporting families. The airlines with the most relaxed atmospheres are probably the best options domestically; and with work culture and employee attitudes in mind, I would lean towards Southwest Airlines, Frontier Airlines, and other small carriers. Through interviews, articles, and websites, the following information might also serve to be helpful.

Southwest Airlines. Offers free family boarding directly after the Priority A boarding group as well as low to no baggage charges. As long as you take advantage of early boarding, you will have ample opportunity to choose seats together on whatever part of the plane you prefer. Activity kits for toddlers are available upon request to help with entertainment needs including Southwest Air Wings. Simple steps are taken to assist parents, such as offering cups that come with lids and straws and offering to assist parents by holding a baby or car seats. Gate passes are granted to parents assisting kids to the gate with some oversight from TSA. Free 'special' beverages are offered to parents flying on Mother's Day and Father's Day. Overall, employees are trained to be family friendly and assist with the travel experience. According to Brandy King, Southwest Airlines Public Relations, "We are all one big family at Southwest, and we always welcome families on board, and do our best to accommodate their travel."

Frontier Airlines. With their slogan "A whole different animal," they pride themselves in being the lowest fare airline that goes out of its way with customer service. With Frontier, you can expect low baggage fees as well as no added cost for preferred boarding for families with children under age three. On their larger planes, Frontier offers Disney movies. Toddlers might enjoy finding a special animal picture on the back wing of the plane. In general, the staff is trained to be supportive of passengers traveling with infants and toddlers and works hard to support all parents' requests.

American Airlines. Offers Admirals Club Children's Rooms, Priority Boarding, and Preferred Seating; but all of these services come at an added cost. In addition, American aims to provide more family-oriented movies during the holiday seasons when more children are traveling. America has a variety of well-known chefs who create a number of "kid-friendly" choices for purchase onboard -- available whether seated in the premium or main cabins. Options range from nutritionally balanced fish, beef and chicken dishes, pasta entrees, turkey sandwiches, cheese and crackers, and ice cream sundaes.

Delta. Like Southwest, Delta also provides kiddie pilot wings. On flights with seatback televisions, Delta offers several On Demand children's television programs at a low cost. Some flights have Nickelodeon and Cartoon Network via satellite television at no additional charge.

United-Continental. Having flown United hundreds of times, I can attest to the fact that United seems to target the business passenger. This is not stated to scare you away, but it is worth noting that the atmosphere on most United flights will be more business than fun. They do offer preferred boarding to children under age four after their priority boarding groups. Snacks and meals are offered at a low cost. And, for the long flights, movies are offered for free, and occasionally are appropriate for children.

In general, you will find that the international airlines are far more accommodating than domestic. This is great news, considering you are likely to have better family support for long international flights. Some examples of the superior accommodations noted by Michelle Higgins in her New York Times Article, *"Are We There Yet?"* include [8.]:

- Dedicated family airport counters and courtesy strollers with **Canada Air.**
- "Carrycots" and infant seats are available with **British Airways** for children up to 2 years old, and "feed kids first" is helpful for hungry toddlers.
- With **Emirates Airlines**, you can expect kids' special backpacks with a children's magazine, puzzles, games, coloring pencils, sleeping mask and a stuffed animal. Also, for babies, jarred baby food and children's menus with items like macaroni and cheese, chicken nuggets, pasta and veggie burgers are available on every flight.
- Menus are kid-friendly and themed onboard giveaways are available for children on **Lufthansa.**

Flying Children with Special Needs

Lisa flies at least once a month on business and several times a year with her children. She has been a unique flight passenger as a result of being in a wheelchair since the age of eight. She continues to fly despite the extra complexity that she faces with her limited mobility. Not only is she one tough cookie, she has clearly mastered flight travel. One of her worst experiences in flight was encountering an experienced flight attendant who found it necessary to incorrectly cover the safety rules with Lisa. It was at this time that Lisa realized the ignorance and insensitivity of people, even those who may be quite experienced in their air travel careers. During her safety debrief this senior flight attendant asked, "In the case of an emergency, do you want to be pulled out by your arms or by your legs???" Fortunately, Lisa knew her rights and the airline policies well enough that she recognized the ignorance of the question and knew the attendant did not know what she was doing. Lisa's advice to others, "Be prepared for ignorance and do your homework so you know your rights and what to expect."

-Lisa Cape Lilienthal, Writing consultant & Mother

It is difficult to travel with typical children, and traveling with children with special needs can provide additional challenges, but it is well worth the time and effort to brave the frontier of travel – for yourself and for your children. Whether your child has mobility limitations, cognitive delays or issues such as sensitivity to loud noises or anxiety in new situations, you can – with planning and support – overcome the limitations and enjoy the experience of air travel. The following section provides useful information on the rights of the disabled and tips to assist them during the unique challenges they face.

The regulatory detail is provided from the website: http://airconsumer.ost.dot.gov/publications/disabled.htm. The Air Carrier Access Act prohibits air travel discrimination on the basis of disability. The Department of Transportation has a rule defining the rights of passengers and the obligations of airlines under this law. This rule applies to all flights on U.S. airlines, and flights to or from the United States by foreign airlines. Airlines may **not** refuse transportation to people on the basis of disability unless carrying the person would be detrimental to the safety of the flight or other passengers. Some of the requirements of the rule include the following:

- Airlines may not require advance notice that a person with a disability is traveling, though carriers may require up to 48 hours' advance notice for certain accommodations such as respirator hook-up.
- Airlines may not require an adult with a disability to travel with another person, except for some very limited circumstances.
- Airlines may not keep anyone out of a specific seat on the basis of disability, or mandate a certain seat assignment on the basis of disability, except to comply with FAA requirements, such as in the case of exit rows.
- **Accessibility of Facilities includes:**
  o New twin-aisle aircraft must have accessible lavatories.
  o New aircraft with 100 or more seats must have wheelchair storage in the cabin.
  o Aircraft with more than 60 seats and an accessible lavatory must have an on-board wheelchair, regardless of when the aircraft was ordered or delivered.

Other Services and Accommodations

Airlines are required to provide assistance with boarding, deplaning and making connections. Assistance within the cabin is also required, but not extensive personal services. Where level-entry boarding is not available, there must be ramps or mechanical lifts to service most aircraft with 19 or more seats at U.S. airports with over 10,000 annual enplanements.

• Disabled passengers' items stored in the cabin must conform to FAA rules on the stowage of carry-on baggage. Assistive devices do not count against any limit on the number of pieces of carry-on baggage. Collapsible wheelchairs and other assistive devices have priority for in-cabin storage space (including closets) over other passengers' items brought on board at the same airport.

• Airlines must accept battery-powered wheelchairs, including the batteries, packaging the batteries in hazardous materials packages when necessary. The airline provides the packaging.

Mobility challenges

When I wrote this book, my thoughts and concerns were focused on the difficulty of flying with young kids, and the underlying assumption was that they were healthy. It was not until I discussed my book topic with a writing consultan Lisa Cape Lilienthal, that I became more aware of the uniqu difficulties faced when a child uses a wheelchair for mobilit

As mentioned above, guidelines exist that prohibit

discrimination against people with disabilities. Although FAA must not discriminate and must accommodate travelers with disabilities, there are some unique considerations when traveling with a wheelchair. The following information was provided by Lisa's observations and experiences:

- All travelers in wheelchairs will require a pat down as part of the security scan, and this may be done a few feet away from your main party. A private screening can be requested. Ensure that you always indicate to the screeners if you have any painful or sensitive areas.

- All bags and wheelchair attachments must go through the x-ray; the wheelchair itself will be patted down as part of the security procedure.

- Airport employees are trained to transfer a passenger from their own wheelchair to a narrow "aisle chair," which will facilitate boarding.

- Airport workers are trained and staffed to provide special assistance such as transporting a passenger via the airport cars.

- Wheelchairs must be stored on the plane before takeoff.

- Passengers with wheelchairs will have the opportunity to board first, and they will be the last to deplane.

- Batteries on wheelchairs will require special storage.

- Most wheelchairs and walkers will be stored in the main cabin. If storage in the cabin is not possible, you will be given a claim ticket at the gate to have the devices stored under the plane.

- Airline attendants will ask if you want assistance once you are boarded.

- During flight, an aisle chair can be requested in the case of needing access to the bathroom. This chair is usually stored near first class. There is commonly one restroom with special accommodations to assist mobility. Attendants can also be asked to help provide privacy near and around the airplane restroom.

- In the event of an emergency landing, flight attendants would put a blanket under you, and passengers would assist with carrying you out.

    Other helpful tips that Lisa mentioned are as follows:

- Aisle seats are necessary.

- Prepare yourself to "roll with it." At times, airport or airline employees can seem ignorant about assisting persons with disabilities.

- Arrive to the airport early, at least one and a half hours before the flight.

    Lisa has been flying for business reasons over several years. And, all in all, she indicated that it is important to be informed as not all employees will be helpful. On the other hand, some individuals will be, according to Lisa, "extraordinary, like Rachel at John Wayne airport who always greets me with a hug and a kiss."

Sensory-challenged

As of the first printing of this book, 1 out of 88 children are diagnosed with autism, and rates of autistic children are on the rise. Sensory challenged children may experience anxiety during a flight – in particular, on takeoff and landing. With heightened procedures at security and while boarding, it does not take much to lead a sensitive child into a state of fear. *Of course, preparation is especially key as children with autism may find it more difficult to adapt to new environments.*

Preparation can be done by:

Taking your child to a small airport beforehand to show them the airplanes and get them accustomed to the noise.

Read books both fiction and non-fiction on airplanes and pilots.

Go on-line and search for pictures that resemble the airline you will be traveling.

- Watch the video "I'm A Good Little Traveler! DVD Toolkit Series: Shae by Air" available at Amazon.com.

Other helpful pointers include:

- Prior to the flight, allow your child to make some choices such as choosing their seats.
- For children who react to loud sounds, investing in better earplugs might be worthwhile, or headsets with a DVD player. Favorite music can go a long way towards calming a child.
- Flying at night might be preferred when sleep is more likely to occur, and minimizing connections is critical so that you minimize the up and downs which will result in less ear popping and less hassle in the aisles.
- Notify the airline that your child has autism and may require special consideration, and on the day of flight ensure security is aware your child has autism.
- To help manage ear and head pressure during takeoff and landing ensure the availability of candy, gum, or favorite snacks.
- Consult your doctor for additional advice. Some doctors will encourage the use of an antihistamine to help calm a child.

Closing

"Two of the greatest gifts we can give our children are roots and wings."

- Hodding Carter

When I was 11, I had my first opportunity to fly on an airplane from Iowa to California. The experience is one that I will never forget, especially the sensation of taking off from the ground and flying above the clouds. While on that trip, I was able to see many of the places that would one day be near my first home in Playa Del Rey, including Venice Beach, Universal Studios, and UCLA. I can't say for sure how much that trip impacted my longing to live in California, but I am sure it had something to do with it. As long as I can remember, I wanted to live in a big city. I would suspect that trips like this first flight ignited my desire to travel and gave me more confidence when the chance to move became an option. Of course, my mom never intended for us to leave Iowa; but on the other hand, she wanted her children to grow up independent and self-sufficient. Having the opportunity to travel to so many diverse places as a child was a major reason why I was able to pursue my dreams of seeing new cities and ultimately build my own life of which my mom is now proud.

Today, I travel with my own children as part of my need to ensure that they know their extended family which spans from Florida to Hawaii. As part of these trips, I also aim to expose them to new experiences and "adventures" as we like to call them. For one day, they, too, will have dreams of their own, unique, free, and only limited by their hearts' desires. Maybe in some way, the trips of today will lend them the confidence to take flight tomorrow.

Bibliography

1.   Flight on-time stats: Website: Bureau of Transportation Statistics, www.bts.gov, http://www.bts.gov/xml/ontimesummarystatistics/src/ddisp/OntimeSummaryDataDisp.xml

2.   Flight Attendant interview: Trish MacDonald, American Air, Oct. 2011

3.   Flight Attendant interview: Shirlee Janson , September 2011

4.   Parent interview: Emily Nelson,, August 6th, 2012

5.   Parent interview: Lisa Lilienthial,, June 8th, 2012

6.   Corporate Communications interview: Brandy King, Southwest Airlines, July 2nd, 2012

7.   Corporate Communications interview: Taylor Hall, American Airlines, June 11th, 2012

8.   Michelle Higgins, Are We There Yet? When Families Fly, New York Times, November 4, 2011

9.   U.S. Travel Association, Travel Facts and Statistics, July 30th, 2012, Travel Horizons Research Project

10.   Sharon, Flight Attendant for 13 years and mother of three, http://flyingwithchildren.blogspot.com/

11.   Shana Draugelis, The Draugelis Blog, The One Where I Get A Smack Down in the Air, May 2012, http://mikeandshanadraugelis.com/2012/05/30/the-one-where-i-get-a-smack-down-on-an-airplane/

Shelley Murasko is a mother of two toddlers who has taken her children into the skies on over a hundred flights. She knows from experience that traveling with young kids can be a challenge; but with the right preparation, mindset and knowledge, flying with young kids can be achieved with ease and joy. By writing this book, Shelley hopes to inspire parents to book that flight and get on their way to building lasting memories with their young children all over this great planet. Shelley resides in Encinitas, CA with her two children, Nolan & Audrey, her husband Mike and her dog, Amigo.

Printed in Great Britain
by Amazon